all the perfect disguises

Poets' Corner Award 2003 judges: Eric Hill, Sharon McCartney, Vanna Tessier
Cover photo and author photo by Allan Neilsen © 2002
Design and in-house editing by the publisher, Joe Blades
Printed and bound in Canada by Sentinel Printing, Yarmouth NS

Also published as BJP eBook 46, ISBN 1-55391-011-7 (PDF)

The publisher acknowledges the support of the Canada Council for the Arts and the
New Brunswick Culture and Sport Secretariat-Arts Development Branch .

Broken Jaw Press
Box 596 Stn A   www.brokenjaw.com
Fredericton NB E3B 5A6   jblades@nbnet.nb.ca
Canada   tel / fax 506 454-5127

National Library of Canada Cataloguing in Publication Data

Neilsen, Lorri
        All the perfect disguises / Lorri Neilsen Glenn.

Poems.
Also published in electronic format.
ISBN 1-55391-010-9
        I. Title.

PS8577.E3373A44 2003   C811'.6   C2003-901685-4
PR9199.3.N35A44 2003

all the perfect disguises

lorri neilsen glenn

Fredericton • Canada

for Grace and Ethel Glenn

All the Perfect Disguises

Shadow's Edge

just as I dance on a Saturday afternoon
in an empty house, for hours sometimes,
all the selves I am ambiguous
and incomplete, as always,
as the same old rhythms rise
and change and relocate themselves,
keeping it up, keeping on
for as long as I do.

— Bronwen Wallace, "Lifelines"

SECONDHAND STORE

Must and the sour odour of decay, frail call of the come and gone, boxed up, stuffed in bags,
into backs of trucks, bottoms of dories, scraped, sanded, shined up with Silvo, nailed, stripped,
folded, crumpled, stocked and stacked at random or in line.

                                      You never know what you'll find.

Could be Ada Arnason's rhinestone earrings, she couldn't tell Howie it was Sarah who
gave them to her on her fiftieth, now lying unclipped near Ernie Coolen's cufflinks, lord,
Ernie Coolen of all people, had either of them known, and

                            there

Silver Birch clustered cup into cup into gravy bowl, like marriage with children, bone
china survivors of Sunday dinners, Thanksgivings, two funerals, three christenings, and that
one time when the schoolteacher dropped by for advice, proud keepers of decorum piece by piece
by steady year assembled by the doctor's wife down near Barss Corner, with one serving plate
remaining, cracked, yes, that time he came back late, that woman from Windsor,
that malingerer, a hint of whisky on his breath and

                         look,

postcards from New York, Bar Harbor, dated 1961: I wish Wayne were here to see
his son, The crossing from Yarmouth was rocky, Mother is well, will write
when I'm settled, *and*

                          these

old boots bent into themselves, tired brown dogs, grey patches of wear, this fellow favoured
one leg, feel how smooth inside, like skin, but wait, he must have felt this tiny nail

                 and this

plain gold band like the one Ethel lost trying to transplant delphiniums, unearthed when
Stanley brought in his backhoe to dig up the garden and drill a new well and it winked
in the sun then was tucked in his overalls, brought back for the daughter living alone
down in Amherst, a baby on the way,

                         and how about

the paisley scarf Inez might have worn in the rain at the platform ceremony in Kamloops,
she was certain Princess Elizabeth glanced at it as she waved, she looked right at Inez, you
know, as the train pulled out, and then the year she went out to see Eunice, left it on a hanger
at the restaurant in Peggy's Cove and the bus nearly left without them, see the pockmarks,
right there, that amethyst pin pushed into the silk so often —
you never know —
detritus and jetsam, silt from the waters of your sedimented life, mute cargo, dumb photographs,
trinkets and frippery and gestures of hearts now absent from body
still as long sorrow,

could be yours, could be mine,
called rudely to assembly, passengers on a ship awakened suddenly by sirens, blinking
in harsh light ragged,
haphazard, aching for place —

unlaced from memory, unravelled
from time,
alien to themselves, beyond
reach of hands to pull them to shore.

White Bones

WALK WITH THE DINOSAURS

In the Fundy museum
old bones settle
behind glass, write
stories to mark them in time: *Mya.*

Mya, 440 to 410, we were silica,
suspension in a shallow Silurian
sea, sensing the presence
of first predators, waiting
on the soft bottom of the warm
floor for time to begin.

What are we but
sand and water, distal fruit
of oceans, rumble and roar,
staring here at our cells under glass,

the tale of our lives told
in silicon rustle, amble and stride.
We exhale the future, everywhere
eyes in a grain of sand.

DELIVERY
Nut Mountain, Saskatchewan, 1909

The horse has drawn the buckboard back from Wadena
in the dark heart of that godforsaken Saskatchewan winter

night, a locomotive of steady flesh delivering again its
whiskey-laced load to the gate, wheezing steam, reins

slack, shrugging off the knock and clink that drew a sharp
line of sound across the hairless skin of frozen prairie. And

stops. Waits, eyelids sewn in ice, until the blink of
light from a lantern stuttering out of the farmhouse brings

the sons, careful not to wake the one inside, now sinking into
night under those old thin covers, her feet pressing stones

warmed on the stove, face and arms free from fists. Let her
sleep. And the horse turns toward their hands, nods, a sign

they tell each other later, it surely was. They probe the stiff
body on board and know, finally, it is over, and their hands

move in dawning unison to lift the reins, leaving vehicle
and man by the gate, high clouds yawning, and lead the beast

out of that brutal wind toward the shelter of the barn.

GLENNIE

Dingle streets, flesh of stones
our bones are sure we knew. While others
comb shops with tourists and locals of a summer mind,
I walk through a small wood door into the sharp
eyes of a stout librarian, smell
the odour of mouldy print.

At the front, encased, the oldest
volumes of uncertain binding,
loose-jointed pages earthy
with promise. Glennie, are you there?

> Mother's mother, small twisted feet
> shuffling down the hall. Bobby-pinned curls,
> barking laugh, walnut knuckles, eyes that swam
> in their own Irish sea.

County Kerry Past and Present. *Handbook to the local
and family history of the county.* Dark red cover. Your hand
reaches through mine, and —

Page 160
Glen, gleann, narrow valley, river course
Glena, baile in Killarney; Lady Kenmore had a cottage
built here amidst fairy scenery
Glenbeigh, birch glen, river in Glanbehy
Glenn, Knight of Fitz Gerald. Ridire an Ghleanna Corbraighe
in Crich Ciarraige, Glin near Tarbert

> Nurse to the few who returned from that war, mother of
> children who scorned, crone of my childhood, Gram
> of my bed-times, friend of the girl you knew I could be.
> Someday, you said.

Glenn na ginci, Glanageenty, in Bally Mac Elligott, 1583
Glenn samaisc, in Templenoe. Glenn scoithin, glen Scota, on sliab Mis,
Glinm baile in Dingle, has forts and cloghauns

Out into the sun, I carry the pages. The song began
here.

At night we climb hills, weave tales into stonecrop
join a chorus of voices calling down an old sea.

PRAIRIE HOME COMPANIONS

Look at all of you:
shuffled, sorted, pinned up with your mothers, unborn
children, sons and sisters, great-nieces, your own
bootied and bonneted infant version, along with those hooligan
friends of your grandchildren, and that damned
daughter-in-law who, you now see,
never aged well after all. Serves her right.
Familia trepidoptera. Homunculi peculiaris.
My gene pool glints back off a wall in the Alberta sun.

So. What have you got to say for yourselves?

And not: *I'd plant more daisies, I wish I'd gone to Australia,*
we never should have left that house on Acadia Bay. Try:

> *You sent me from Kamsack to have the child alone and hand him to*
> *the nuns. It was forty years before he found me.*

> *Leonard, if you'd kept it in your pants your children would be with you now*
> *and you wouldn't be wandering Polo Park Mall at eighty carrying*
> *shopping bags for that shrew.*

> *Did I ever tell you why I was afraid of going early to prepare for mass?*

> *I'm sorry I left you and your brother with the MacDonalds afterward.*
> *But I was lonely, frightened, hopeful, and your father died so young.*

> *You should have married those fucking dogs instead of me. I hated them:*
> *they slobbered and they stank.*

> *Yes, she was Cree, but we didn't talk about that, not then.*

And: *You saved me. I took your friendship to my grave.*

We need a wake for us all, a roaring
barbecue in a prairie field. Come as you are,
corsets and top hats, canes and old lace, dirty
knees and Kiwanis parade costumes.
Bring the old Studebaker. Come
as you are, were, and will be,
would and should and could have been.
Bring your favourite trait, your most generous gene, bring your absent present:
the snow that fell on the new barn, the spray from Athabasca Falls, the songs
you sang at the cradle, the sweet peas from Eleanore's yard. Bring the liminal

as liquid to drink straight up, and we'll walk the yellowed pasture, watch
embers light our eyes around the circle, coals to stoke
from dusk until dark,
ash for an articulate dawn.

CIRCLE GAME
for and after Joni Mitchell, John Smyth, Monsieur Hinitt and the last Aden Bowman reunion

In the foyer, wide hips in new clothes, well-groomed painted
ponies of the past, a quiver
lifting under our ribs, eyes in careful check,
through bifocals at the strange familiar
under glass, dragonflies captive
in a jar, every howling blemish, lacquered backcomb job, lazy greasy lock of hair,
and the seasons,
round and round

turn cartwheels through the town, accordion pleats of a skirt, scissoring
limbs in October air, sixteen springs and sixteen summers gone,
captive in the circle game,
wooden desks and thumb-finger paper fortunes opening, closing, up,
down, white beaks of promise, we can only look
behind from where we came,
go round, go
round.

142 Tucker Crescent Saskatoon Saskatchewan Canada the world the planet
the solar system the universe, the falling of a star, red wine of desire
on our tongues, hands bristling fingers, dashboards and porch lights, lips
plucking nipples drawing up, drawing
words like when you're older, better
dreams and plenty,
captive on the carousel, round and round, rings
wrapped with Johnson's tape, sealed with polish, painted ponies, up,
down, promises of some day, Theseus, theorems, Hippolyta hypothesis,
Puck and précis, up, out, Eddie, Pat, Edna, Mardi, Mel, Dale, Carol, Wayne gone
into cars, seasons of arms, longing, limbs, birthing, bearing, coupling,
uncoupling, dying, and
dying still. Round and round

behind glass, teachers young then as our own children now,
how we laughed, tidy shirts, thin sweaters, saddle shoes, wan conviction,
their vague after-school lives, careful messages from out there, their algorithms
of time, calculations of interest, theses for essays into life.

19

But here, turned by years, old gatekeeper of Shakespeare, fierce lord
of English, noble jaw, granite eyes, dispenser of spittle, soliloquy, prophecy —
Joan Anderson will never amount to anything —
captive in sinew, curled like tree roots, a whisper
in the hallway, his last revolving year.

And the seasons, round and round, painted ponies
lost, found, lives, dreams, grandeur, sky,
thunder, we can only look,

go round and round, and
wonder at the coming true.

FIRST MEMORY

Silver jaws of its grille, my mother
running — *I must have wandered* — jaws
of a monster roaring out of dust — *outside*
the gate — jaws, the grille — *away, pulling*
sky with me — a man opening
a door above my head — *pulling sky to the road* —
grey door opening like a wing — *drawn to the heat* —
voices, hands — *heat of the road* —
jaws, the monster and
me
on my back
flesh knuckled with stones, drunk
on my senses, fists stuffed with
imminence,
tongue
tasting cloud.

BEAR LAKE

He carries me high
in the crook of his elbow, my bare legs
like dry fish, my arms rope around his neck,

and I thrill at the terror below, metal scent
of water cold in my nostrils, want not to cleave
(his naked shoulder new and strange), and the lake
splashes at my feet, drops fat as horseflies that hover,
                                        snarl.
And Jeanie next to me, her father's blond curls,
we dangle eye to eye above Bear Lake, six-year-olds
with men we did not know
were so young, our new bodies fresh
streams of their eternity, and they bend toward water now,
laugh, release,
tighten their grip,
                bend again,
                    squint into the eye of the Brownie.
We peer under the sun-lanced surface for their feet, shapes that ripple,
dark swirls we've been told are tiny creatures,
bloodthirsty thrusting
things, names new
to the tongue.

Perhaps that's how it was. And Lillian laying the blanket under the spruce
near the fire pit, lighting a Players as she adds kindling, bats at mosquitoes,
unwraps the egg salad sandwiches sweating mayonnaise in the heat,
her ear tuning for applause

of the bullet-grey surface
when bodies strike, limbs explode

into spray, but instead hearing only my mother, camera poised, calling:

Al, Jim, don't frighten them.

The knot on my swimsuit strap bites my neck, ruffled cotton pinches
between my legs. I want
                              down
from his warm skin angry flies rutting heat of the sun
want fingers of cold water crawling down my back, want it all, take
the picture, hold me up then let me drop, shoot for the bottom, stroke
my own burning bones in depths that mottle my skin, arouse my hungry

legs, there are raw things
wet gnawing eruptions

I do not know I
need to name.

THE DRESS, FROM HERE
A response to C. K. Williams

In those days, those days that come back to you now and then when your
       body tells it
all unwittingly, triggered by the neighbour's morning greeting as you
       shake
the rug and smack the broom against the porch, or by the apprehension
       of your mother's

face glaring back at you at night, your brush in hand; in those long-ago days
       when you
awoke to scrapes of spoons in bowls, refrigerator handle kachunk, ka-
       chunking,
and the brittle crack on arborite of milk brought down again like a brick,
       full stop,

days the odour of Old Spice led from the bathroom directly out the door, when
       the last
sound at night was the snap of your transistor radio tuned into yearning,
       having
known since you were ten that grieving life is worse than grieving death, and you
       wanted

your chest, strung tight on wires of silence, someday to be played loose, like
       the blues;
but all you knew was the sway of her housedress as she walked away in one of
       those many
shapeless cotton prints that covered the mystery of your birth, slack fleshy
       parts

your mouth and hands once sought, apparently, and location, you suspect,
       of confusing
late night rhythms down the hall. In those days, those days when cap guns,
       jacks,
evie-ivy-over and the basket of books you wheeled home every week from
       the library

told you little of women and men or how to tell the story in starched shirttails
　　　burned
after dark or egg-stained housecoats worn all day or curlers wound for no
　　　occasion but
clean hair, and how tight mouths, loose clothes, the red end of a cigarette
　　　in the dark

wrote, in those days, a language of refusal it would take you forty years to read.

MOP THE FLOOR

Ad in the Student Union that spring: *Psych. aide. Weyburn, min. wage, room and board.*

Second week learn the rhythm, seven and one-quarter hours underground tunnels meals long steel tables, learn sodden trails of a mop twisted creatures at the end of old men's legs corns, drool warm water soak pus-eyed toes in buckets they tip, learn

to laugh with them and

pass by trembling limbs against cement walls bucking bucking, empty eyes, return with clean clothes now, mop lift the ones with lightning shot through veins out of straps into the bath, heads bobbing lolling travellers in uncharted galaxies bearing light their own starry night.

Hold the horizon and the handle,

watch Joe, little Joe back from surgery, they pulled out shoelaces cigarette butts tin wrappers twigs (so that's where...) smokes snatched from the nursing station tobacco still burning Joe sucking furiously red light flaring sparks down to the end, suck suck suck and then — gone down his gullet.

Find home in asylum,

at seventeen a mop is not heavy, 6:55 a.m. sharp out the residence door into the open, uniform a clean page, nylons white screen in sunlight, shoes wiped bright with sponge wick swipe mop urine clay infielder mashed potatoes gloss a floor that bears the weight of groan and bellow and bay,

mark fresh landscape

with vestal eyes and good intentions. Wipe hold feed bathe mop, want only that Joe laugh, Harold's foot fit into his shoe today, the crying stops, that Hank and Doreen don't leave the grounds again hide naked in the bushes, that a paycheque waits at 3:30. Walk up and out through the catacombs, join

a boy in his Impala drive until dusk to the outskirts of town silver pails of
meteors tipped across the sky, horizon an ocean mop a mast, tomorrow as crisp
as hospital issue as generous as dawn, surge, run ahead, sweep away fingers of
cirrus, limbs of cumulus, whiskers of dust, apparitions of

the roil and chill that wait below.

VOLUNTEER

He is dying. All skin, organs,
and history of him. There is nothing
to do. She arrives every day
at the same time. They smile
past each other, she takes the tray.
He has learned if he is regular
with pills and bowels
and tales of his war,
she will survive.

LUCKY

bends into the drugstore counter at closing time, bratwurst
fingers working the worn leather of his change purse — *here's a*

loonie — dealt on the glass in a flourish, like the ace
of spades, and now a quarter, flip of the wrist,

another. One more. *One seventy-five? Can't hear*
anymore, you know. Cashier smiles, enunciates. Hands him

the receipt. He nods, eyes down, erupts in guttural thanks,
pushes at pockets with his blunted slabs. And then

the chocolate is on the floor, sleeves of the bars sliding
off foil, he doubles over, pawing at the tiles, grey hair sweeping,

carnival nickel digger now, shovel sifting air. I kneel
to help but — magical — he has shuffled them, briskly

stacked the wrappers one on one, scooped them
into his bag, into the pocket of his hand-knit jacket, stuffed

the cache into how many other moments, seasoned croupier at
this crap table, the fix in, slouching now toward the exit, borne

into darkness, clock above the locking door ticking
even though we cannot see its face.

MUIR WOODS: YEARS LATER

You have not been back since the day you wore rain
and the hands of ferns blessed the ground, since

you were supple, receptive as the forest floor. Later
on the Sausalito ferry you showed him the blood you drew

on the tallest redwood. Scored by the tree's rough
flesh, your hand still carries the scar, a promise, perhaps,

or a pact with time. You were born again that day in desire,
shuddered at the thought of dying young. Now, you seek

the safety of old trees, their steady grace under the urgent sun.
You don't invite their marks, but work beside them

inhaling light, peeling back years, taking root from
long green afternoons.   But

Oh,
that wild pain those wet woods sinking moss green bed,
tremor of limbs mouths damp insinuating leaves reckless
fingers, innocence of branches snapping, how you opened,
rising
to the skin of
everything.

DAYS BEYOND

Ah, this flesh, once taut and tightly thrumming
a song of rolling nights, each word a tincture of iron,

each tune the hungry breath of wolves, and on your tongue
the tang of ancient salt, your limbs unnamed comets, you

looked into a glass the way you walked into an ocean, blithely
ablaze, humming white at the centre. And your mind, ah,

the torque in that force, a million cubic pathways, a labyrinth,
grip of an eagle's talon, wet eye of crocus, howl of steel

on stone, and sparks, yes sparks, electric sky in June,
alchemy, turbid pain and ravenous laughter, your mind:

Christ, what couldn't you know then. A bloody angel you were.

To lay a sheet down at the edge of the earth now,
heart ticking its numbered days, no one seeking

redemption between your legs, picking your mind
like morning crows, to lie suspended over the abyss, feel

the pulse of a stranger approaching on a path
unknown to you, bearing ink, words as water, words

as host, your bodies whispering down sand as that tangerine
magnet sweeps the sky, lifts the hands of the sea

to the chalice of your mouths.

FIRE
for Catherine Kennedy, great-grandmother

Métis country wife
a hundred years away, ablaze

on a riverboat off Warren Landing,
you bore demands

of Catholic clerics, a French prospector,
and eleven of his children.
                              Only six survived
you. Incinerated
on a northern lake,

worth an inch in *The Free Press*,
not a word in my home.

At twelve, I knew, looking
at those brown girls hiding

at the back of history
class in The Pas,

bones aflame
cast light through

time: your eyes, this photograph,
my mirror.

THE CLEAN LIFE

Washing up dishes after dinner with my cousins (there is a right
way to dry them and to soak a pan), holding my brother's diapers

tight in icy water as I flush the toilet, swirl the cloth to loosen
shit. Washing up beer my boyfriend spills, ashtrays overturned

in a fight, the cold sticky remains of our greedy coupling in the back
of the car, on his parents' couch, on the rug in his sister's apartment. Washing

up clay the pimply man-boys fling on the classroom wall,
plates and cups in the staff room during my spare while science teachers

play Yahtzee, snort at jokes. Washing up the newly-painted
bathroom before in-laws come for dinner, the kitchen floor before

the landlord stops in, the car dashboard, copper dish, hairy gum
deep in the drain, and the vegetable crisper just in case.

Washing out the siennas and sepias of baby diarrhoea, drippings, droolings
and blood shot from a gash over an eye when he tore off on the new bike, did
a wheelie, then a face plant, and the doctor — so young — hands shaking, left gravel
in his temple sewn in like a grimace.
                              Washing up needles when the Christmas tree
goes up and when it comes
down, and weeks afterward, the ones left when I thought I'd got
them all. A quarter century of pots in a great lake of water
and splash tracks on the mirror.
                              Washing bottles for the recycling bin and chocolate
on the piano keys, digging in their ears where they cannot see, wiping away
the paste under foreskin they must learn about. Smudges on my eyeglasses, and
now, more than ever, the windows overlooking the cove in early autumn. You see,
the sun hits dead on sometimes, exposes streaks on the pane,
        scurf of long summers —
                expeditions of spiders, trepidations of moths, the salt
                of sea spray, silica dust, all of it, and the whole earth tilts,
bending my view.

KITCHEN

1
The door opens
to spring air at the cabin.
A crow caws.
Coffee gurgles in the making, I smell
the threat of memory. Down the hill, the neighbour's
hammer and saw, a sudden slam.
           Slam.   The kitchen door. The cupboard. Her keening,
                               his sullen silence. My brother's wide eyes.
(Knock knock
Who's there?
family at the kitchen table
broccoli boiled past yellow, pork chops
seared. We hide words under our
tongues, point the knives away
from our hearts.)

Saturday afternoon at the theatre, music and hot horses carry me into dust
and open sky. I am Annie Oakley, riding past a backdrop I painted. On Jeanie's back
stoop under high Alberta clouds we drink Kool-Aid, cut a wardrobe with press-back
tabs for Betty and Veronica, cardboard dreams bought for a dime. Inside the red
brick school, smooth pink reassurance of an eraser, industry of woody
shavings, taste of the word *foolscap* and primary colours in the land of Dick and Jane
and ways to stay within the lines.
                           After,
in the kitchen, I concentrate on reading the silence,
writing *courage* inside my veins.

Here, it is still too cold to plant
vegetables, too wet. I will
drink my coffee, watch the tide, listen
to the neighbour clatter and slam,
leave the kitchen door open
to a tentative sun.

Out on the Fundy mud flats the red earth
shifts and what flows out today could
be anywhere tomorrow.

2
Every Christmas he sends small cheques
in one of those cards for giving money rather
than attention. The older
boy spends his ten right away. The
younger, who has never seen the man,
leaves his with me.

I could buy a toy with the money, I suppose, listen to my six-year-old
vroom vroom around the kitchen table where my father
once sat, head in his hands and said: I'm warning you. I'm leaving her. I'll be
gone next year.
                         Or I could put the money in the bank,
watch it grow, turn the seasons like compost
toward light, weed out filaments of memory, those
urgent bursts of green.

3
He polishes the hood,
stopping now and then to dig
the cloth into the can
of wax. The dog
on the grass
watches a fly.

From the step my neighbour appears, calling
her father in to eat. Her frame fills the doorway
with the unborn grandson, her belly high and wide.
                 Oh
I remember
how full that was.

His hands on the car
moving
back and forth
back and forth, a
backrub,
                    a long embrace.

The finish gleams snow white, sun spun. The grandfather-to-be
stands back, admires his work.
The dog rises.

From my kitchen window, I cradle
a coffee cup. It has been more than the lifetime
of my youngest child since I have seen
my father's face,
heard him
say my name.

4
You have cancer —

curable, an operation,
you thought I ought to know.
Your voice lifted on lines from the prairie to my kitchen
on the coast is tired, crumbles
not with emotion, but
years of use.

How many words
you did not speak to me
                    and now
only these?

In three minutes, the
call is over. You avoid
my questions, ask me
only one.
            Yes, the boys are fine.

Damn you.
These moments rob the grave where I buried the skinny morning
girl, jam pail of blueberries, smell of spruce gum, my name, in baritone,
Annie Oakley's six-gun.

I'll tell my doctor
to add more history to the chart.
Throat, stomach,
lungs, colon,
heart.

DRIVING ON

He ran the red light. Beside him,
she gasped: Where are you
going? He shrugged, drove on
home, offered only
a benign smile.

At dinner, his grandson stared at his
mouth, cocked his head, turned
to his own father for the answer
no one had.

Later, in the basement, his son found him
alone under a light at the workbench,
duct-taping the old tools together,
wrapping a runaway world.

Where is my wallet? Who are you?

On their fiftieth she wore her
going-away dress, asked friends to dinner.
When he broke conversation
in his teeth, bouncing words like pearls
off the waxed wood floor,
she picked them up,
smiled, served the salad. She knew
everyone would understand.

But the engine of his mind began
misfiring that year, blurted chaos
with a force that wanted only connection,
hearing. She listened, brought him
pills, made roast beef, his favourite, drove
him to the doctor, phoned about
the tests. He went in overnight for
a simple operation, and for the first time
in months she slept.

The bed was still, the furnace
idled and sighed, the basement wrapped
in rings of silver tape.

Safe, she thought.
At least he hadn't wandered off, been
found confused and cold. Hadn't rolled
up on shore, bloated with sea water, gulls
rasping like sirens on the rocks.
The next morning, the doctor's
voice: He's staying on.

Last week she signed
all the papers:

The red lights
are everywhere and his mind
is running them all.

COVER STORY

1

Upstairs on the bureau fat snowflake doilies, a basin
and pitcher of rose-ringed bone china. At ten, I spied
through lace on the window, imagined carriages and horsemen
on steam-snorting steeds. My grandmother's quilt lay like blue snow

in twilight, bedposts were lamps guiding nights
on the farm. In sleep I heard goose down crackling like grassfire,
the delicate cover as wan as her cheek. Mornings we shook
out the quilt and the pillows, and our laughter shot feathers

into cold early light.

2

At twenty,
        I tossed it
into the back seat
of a borrowed convertible,
drove all night
over the mountains
to Wreck Beach,
a fire, Country Joe and the Fish on eight-track,
he and I writhing on cool sand,
cloaked in down
and skin.

3

For years I dropped feathers, bits of down floating around the base
of the Rockies, scattered on highways, pressed into the floorboards
of a flat off Seventeenth, a house on Richmond Road. One August day
I fought with fabric, needle glanced by the sun, stitching
a second skin of red velour to stay the flow of aimless
drifting white. What did I know
of balance? The feathers clumped then and twisted
like Rasta coils trapped under a hat.

4
Today I drag it from the basement
to take to the cabin with other
strays. It holds the promise of warmth,
warmth of old promises, stories

in skin I lay on the bed.

                But it will not spread, will not
                lie flat, flops in a lump, an old
                        body curling, resisting
                my grasp. I lift, shake it. At the seams
                        quill ends rise, tiny
                                white bones pierce
                                        the red flesh.

Moonskin

IN RETREAT
For Joan Clark and the Rogersville writers

1
Train whistle. Ravenous
jaw of night opens,
swallows raw dreams.

2
The field remembers
the tractor, said the nun,
how can you forget god?

Monarch escorts me
through hot summer field, whispers
last night's psalm of rain.

Cat on blinking buttercups,
belly to the sun.
Yes, it is enough.

3
Mon Dieu! A wimple
as simple as sunlight,
habit of June air.

4
In the quiet chapel,
summer storm of words,
washing a tender Word.

5
Women turning earth
together in the abbey,
harvesting a life.

Women turning words
together in the abbey,
harvesting a life.

6
What daisies know
of epistemology
they write with petals.

7
At compline song
sighs down the day,
wrap of pure white.

At dusk a train calls.
Daisies wave an answer.
Believing is enough.

FEMINIST THEORY

is written also in late September, on a day with a breeze, a touch
of ice in the air,

a day when you walk to the beach, search for plants and shells,
return at dusk to a darker room

for soup, a bit of wine, a book, and sleep,

never once having to question
a shadow or a sound.

EASTER BREAK

In the kitchen
my mother and sister
clatter plates.
Dinner waits on Bible study.

A spring wind outside ruffles
dark water running blue
under the sun. Upstairs,

Uncle Ernie's
suitcase is by the bed,
his good book on the table.
His fingers roam

my damp shirt, rub
my April flesh.
The window is open
to the water below.
Rye breath on my back

heaves like winter wind
coming back. Coming
back. Again.
Again.
The curtains try to leap
off the sill,
melting ice hammers
nails on the roof. The wind
groans, swells

up from the river where
floes crack. Four limbs
across my great aunt's
wooden bed, hard
hard and harder, rise
and rising. I float, search

through the glass, paint
a brown patch for a
blood red robin, draw thistle
near the riverbed, imagine
a place to go to rock
the ache. Burning pulls
me down, down,
his breath, the wind —
oh, jesus,
howling jesus, jesus,
jesus,
jesus, sweet
girl, the
power and
the glory.

CHECKOUT

— Listen to this: "The body was stuffed in the dishwasher. The skin, spongy and swollen, filled the corners of the machine. When the door was opened, the victim's arm fell over the edge like a wet sock." Jesus, how do they think of these things?

— Remember the one hung upside down in the hotel room, throat slashed, all the blood drained out through the ceiling below. I mean imagine finding that, eh?

— That was an old *L. A. Law*, I think. Are you going to buy this?

— You're right. And what about the one raped in front of her daughters and beaten to death with one of those hammers, you know, for pounding chicken — no, I'm not, can't afford it. I just read them here, in the line — pulverized. Right in front of the kids. That was no TV show. That really happened.

— Mallets, they're called. And then there's these weirdos who skin them like animals — what was the name of that movie with what's-her-name, Jodie Foster? — Oh, god, look at the time. I'm gonna be late getting supper again. Here, if you're not buying this, I will. Payday.

— How's your arm?

— It's fine. I'll be fine. You know me. Mouthy.

— They found that missing girl, you know. Remember her mother came out from B.C. to search for her? Her head was in one part of the woods and her body in another. God love her. They think she was picked up by those pimps.

— Come on. I've got to get the potatoes on. Call me later, when he's at the pub.

CH'I
for Daphne Marlatt

In-
tend, as the muscle of reed bears
down in the water, toeing
in, shouldering

the wind. Drift, as a vessel
cupping cargo drops
a plumb for sway

& swing. Like fish

dart from predators that come at
you. Breathe out what
rises from your gut.

Consume no alphabetic
truths, they eat you
from within. Wave

at theory: dry & snug on shore,
it sucks up heat,
evaporates. Breathe in &

                           turn
away from shoal
to dip & curve in wind
& bend & roll
& watch   your heart:
now in your hand   it trembles,
now in the air   it flies

                    alone, alone.

A FEW MORE WORDS ABOUT BREASTS
for Mary Schoeneberger and Margie O'Brien

Naked and cleaning the bath, my hand
bumps my breast
and pain soars. It's the season
when my body is changing
rhythm, when red tides heave what remains
of the moon's possibilities.
A season to struggle
with time, fatigue,
fresh aching.

I stand and cradle it, skin
smooth as floured silk, heft
of butter softened for the dough.
Nipple pliable, curled down from use.

Poking, kneading, probing now,
I cannot know
what the tides have washed in
these many years. Or will.
Lumps? None yet. Only knots
of pain throbbing
deep into my arm.

Outside, leaves are lit by October sun. Summer is leaving
my body. The bitter fruit in my hand is

moonskin marking the long journey into winter.

HIGHER EDUCATION

You stand across the doorway
of your office, giving
audience, nodding,
nodding. Just so.

Middle-year co-eds, frightened
by rumours of the desert out there
wait to drink from your tongue. Hard
round lips jut naked
from your soft beard,
poised, like your feet, in position
just, just so.

O, patriarchy! The women
weep: It is not just. O,
hegemony! No truth,
no justice.
Nodding, mouth O-
racular, you give
good confession. They wail,
touch your wordbeads,
wipe their tears, bless you
for your time.

I close my
door on that altar, open
the window, watch
the moon sail
over hallway gods.

AIR TIME

He looks at his watch, the seatbelt sign,
the flight attendant, his watch, then
his eyes fire wide wild shots
in my direction.
Glances at the time
again. Again. His
shoulders shudder,
feet hop, doing
the seat jive.

Outside, in the grey January air
trucks circle the plane,
a man in a bucket sprays green
and blue liquid on the wings.
The pilot calls last check.
The man starts, shakes,
his feet two-stepping.
The watch, again. Shakes
his arm, jerks his collar, shoots
his cuff, checks the time.
Once more the dance.

I feel his crazy
emu eyes
on my page,
my face.
I pray,
let's get this damn thing
off the ground. Now

comes the unbidden
torrent of words: his books,
religious studies, his stay
in Toronto, on a fellowship
and no one — no one! — asked him to
dinner, coffee. Nothing! Six months!

Nothing! The costly renovations
to his home. Buddhism, a cash cow,
and he, I ought to know, among the first
to milk it. I nod,
mention the growing numbers
of Buddhists in my community. He corrects me,
adjusts his collar, shakes his sleeve,
glances and glances
at the work in my lap, gives
me the reference for
his latest book.

Aloft now, I am a gull, flying near a twister.
An eagle, circling a fire. A dove, waiting
out the storm. Steady,
in the air, on my own.

FLYING WITH FOUCAULT

As I stand in the courtyard with my glass
of passable red and shift
from hip to hip, watching
jaws like rucksacks
empty news of lengthening c.v.,
last keynote address, cost of the new Saab,
name of a good therapist, caterer,
contact for the dearest villa in Tuscany you've ever seen
and — sotto voce —
the goddamned Judas at the last faculty meeting what the hell was that about —
                                                            as I watch

eyes dart about for fatter crudités,
tastier conversation, more
well-connected ears —
excuse me, I just have to talk to him about the edits on my article —
                        as water rises, fills the cracks between stones,
                    pulls in goatees, pigs in blankets, broccoli
                    flowerets and sensible shoes, sucks in
                    vests, pot bellies, hummus,
                    limbs in urban black leather,
                                soaks the courtyard,
                    churns an epistemological soup,
                        a post-post potpourri, rising, rising,
            I strip right down
                        to my feathers,
            fly to the corner of the building,
                    alight in the ivy,
            pick my wings clean of ticks
            and dirt and the detritus that swarms in bad air,
                            then settle in, watch
                            as eddies swirl below,
                            tables crumble,
                            glasses shatter, and

just as the water licks
at my panoptical perch,
    I lift,
        spread my wings,
                roll
            into the slipstream,
soar
      into clear sky.

IT'S HARD TO BELIEVE

that scientists cut the vocal cords of laboratory cats.
That crocodiles are born with internal clitoral
penises. That snow flies, words
kill. It's hard to believe shops in the mall are stocked
with colour, odour, soundtrack
because science shows what sensory signals fire
our desire to flash a credit card, lick a label, feel the fabric, do the lifestyle.
A criminal offence in Canada to clone a human. But then came Dolly
to heat the blood of every pointy-headed lab rat dreaming
a perfect control group. Men and sheep, again. Ah, wake up, little
Suzie. The brazen ewe of our conscience has been strolling the market
for years, waddling her daggy buttocks into Martha's kitchen, fleecing
Oprah's book display, sucking a half caff decaff
with us at Starbucks. And we balk when she asks us
to make an honest ewe
·of her?

CARMEN

wears plastic
see-through shoes,
paints her toenails
red fire.
Tanned skin,
veins blue
wire beneath
fine clay.

Hip bone
juts in slick black
pants. She turns in the
chair her other
hip sharp. Flips
one leg across the knee,
quick as a chirp.
Brown shoulders
straight, firm,
clavicles sculpted,
fifty years of angles,
control.

Blinks.

Carmen's black roots
dance in bottle
red, strands cut
pin-precise.
Nails pressed
to cheekbone.

After the war,
she says, we
escaped Europe.
We've lived
on three continents
since.

I search this
storied face,
these stark eyes.

At the edge
of my chair,
I listen as
words like
clockwork click
from her
tongue, hear
shrill silence,
birds humming
on a wire
ready to scatter
in the crackle
of Carmen electric.

AT UGLY DUCKLINGS ANONYMOUS

My turn? Uh, okay, my name is Annie, and I think it began when my
boyfriend's sister laughed at me. Hippy hippie she called me and I guess I was
wider than her, well, a bit, with more hair, and in different places, but at least
my toenails didn't scream in Fisher Price colours and I never blew two weeks'
wages on make-up — you can buy six books for the price of a beauty system,
they call them systems now — never treated myself to lunch and eyelash dyeing
with my mother. C'mon, some women's lips are always so slick you'd think they
owned their own Zamboni, and their hair treated, permed and frosted — I
mean, pay someone 100 dollars to put tinfoil on it? — and speaking of hair, I
never, ever, owned a hairdryer, I mean why bother? Air is free.

So I have a problem, I know it. I understand that some women need to pull out
a mirror every time they have a new face to greet, but I don't. Well, sometimes,
when I have to drive to the Save-Easy for bread I'll grab the lipstick I keep
in the bathroom drawer, same one for years, but that's all. And maybe a little
eyeliner, just a dab. If I can find it. These things can get out of hand, and before
you know it, bingo, there you are, well into your pension years with yellow hair
and blue eyelids, trying to close the fake gold clasp on your white shorts,
looking for chips in the purple polish on your toes, which, by the way, look like
scraps of leather, and reaching for your wallet with claws for hands — you
know you can get sparkles for your fingernails now? — looking
for all the world like a Disney lizard. And what have you got?
Well, not your dignity, that's for sure.

And so what, so what if men look right
through me like I'm a hedge or a lamppost — and when they do look they
probably think Birkenstock Bertha or something. Well, fine. The ones that do
make eye contact always look like the kind who spend hours browsing through
a bookstore or working on a crossword or sitting by the water talking, which is
my style, really, not sitting by the pool in Florida waiting for the free pink
drinks and the bus trip to the casino, and everything smelling like chlorine and
Estee Lauder. Phew.

So, okay, so that's
how I feel. I'm not, like, proud of it. But you won't see me ordering those
ceramic dolls with teardrops in women's magazines, and I don't think rat-sized
dogs should wear doll clothes and I can't say Mary Kay without wanting to
burp — or am I thinking of Tupperware?— and I just don't get this thing about
collagen and silicone. Who wants lips like a llama or tits that don't roll over

when you do? I'm tired of baby boomer Barbies, slathered in goop tested on animals, advertising huge corporations on their backsides, still longing for that perfect little black dress. I mean, really.

Okay, I'll stop.

No, wait.

Maybe it's personal. Maybe it all started in the school washroom in grade nine when Cherie Libbrecht stood there squinting into the mirror. She had a contraption your big toe would fit inside of, and I stood there, flat-chested with my ponytail, braces and all, my chunky mouth wide open, as she pointed this, this Thing, at her face. Isn't that a toenail clipper? I asked, and suddenly the walls were echoing guffaws, all the wide open red mouths. Squawking teenage crows with lipstick, they were, and even my best friend Sandra was hooting from the stall, and I was standing alone, confused, with the scent of Noxzema on my skin and a too-tight elastic tweaking my hair.

Later I learned that gizmo was an eyelash curler.
But you knew that, I bet.

Okay, I'm done. Your turn.

POET IN THE HOUSE: A HANDBOOK

A. Pest Control:

If you are infested with vermin, but know a poet, you are in luck. Poetry will drive rats and mice from a house. Rats, especially, have an aversion to rhyme. Jot a poem on a sheet of paper, place it beside cracks in the baseboards near openings to the ground below, and the creatures will flee to the homes of neighbouring curmudgeons. This never fails. Of course you must be a friendly neighbour yourself. What goes around, comes around, as you have heard.

B. Percussion:

Poets were once called beats for a reason. Ask a poet to join your garage band or your Saturday blues jam. The vein of poetry, located at the back of the poet's head, begins to throb with the metre of the emerging poem. You have a choice of beats: iambic, dactylic, anapestic, elastic, iconoclastic, dipsomaniacal. Gaelic poets worked in darkness, so you might first place the poet in a nearby cupboard. And you might at first stick to something simple — "Louie Louie," perhaps, or an instrumental by Duane Eddy. In the interests of maintaining a good relationship with your neighbours (see A, above), avoid anything by ABBA.

C. Budgeting and Property Management:

A poet is well-versed in creative ways to scrimp, save, barter, and borrow. He will be able to advise you on the five-dunk teabag; turnstile-jumping; automobile-sharing; dumpster-diving with dignity (tip-robbing, in Great Britain); gift-giving (poetry as economical birthday, anniversary, St. Patrick's Day present); and wardrobe enhancement (how to turn a luxury item, such as a sheepskin jacket, a pair of steel-toed boots, or an Aran Island sweater, into community property). A poet is particularly skilled in the art of bartering unwanted possessions (a Sinéad O'Connor CD or that vase from the aunt) for more useful or necessary items. If you contract the poet to do some of your bartering, be clear about your expectations from the start. Poets are inclined to list under 'necessities' items such as single malt, a spliff, good red wine, and fine chocolate.

D. Investment and Financial Planning:

Not applicable.

E. Home Maintenance and Repair:

See Investment and Financial Planning, above.

F. Family Planning Or How to Conceive Your Own Poet:

Poetry is a hereditary gift that abandons a family for seven generations if bestowed on a female. Historically, there have been fewer female than male poets, unless you include 'Anon,' which some claim is a generic pseudonym for women. The best advice, then, is to bear only sons. If you are determined to conceive a female poet, you may increase your chances by taking three steps:

1. With your partner, leap over the edges of fires (preferably Bealtaine fires) to ensure fertility.

2. Find a fasting poet to spit on you: spittle is a person's undiluted essence and confers special powers.

(These steps give you the luck of the Irish to begin. Note: a child born with a caul — the cap of happiness — is blessed with good fortune, and a child born on Sunday has a saintly character suitable for the creation of inspirational works, but such children do not always become poets. Do not depend on the practice of dreaming of what you want for three nights running. Belief in the prophetic dream has its merits, but it has thus far proven unreliable with regard to potatoes in the nineteenth century, Michael Collins' longevity in the twentieth, and peace in the twenty-first. What is certain is that December 28th, the day commemorating the slaughter of the Holy Innocents, is, by far, the unluckiest day of the year. Plan with care.)

3. Give birth on or near the stroke of midnight. Without this timing, no female child ever becomes a poet.

Carry her early and often to the top of the hill at the edge of the sea
where she will draw inspiration from the land and the water below.
When she is of an age to speak, the force of gravity from this height
lends weight to her
    words and these
            words — sure as the head
              on your Guinness, sure as
            the gates of Kilmainham,
              sure as fish on Friday and a
            tiff by the Liffey on a Saturday night — these
               words will
                        drop,
        like songs of
        stone, jack-knifing
        fairies, catapulting
        angels,
            like serendipity,
        into the rushing
        rollicking sea.

[1] The superstitions referred to in this poem are described in Daithi o Hogain's *Irish Superstitions* (Dublin: Gill & Macmillan, 1995)

Shadow's Edge

HERE

The birch dangling gold asks for your eyes.
A stone, your warm hand. The snow,
nakedness and blood. And the doe drawing
taupe lines against the hill wants your breath,
deep, slow, inaudible.
You want nothing.

Later in the crowd at dinner, she said, I saw you on your balcony.
He said, Get a life. I'm not that interesting. The room
full of empty noise. You
know nothing.

Now you are at your window. Tree waving,
wind calling all the names of the world. Sun
stretches around every peak in the valley. Here
now is the man, not on the balcony, but in the pines
below. Alone, focusing a lens. He does not see you.
You are not there.

Snow, sun, tree, glass, doe, man, woman, blood, stone.
Who sings you here? Who listens?

Sky is a blue language, earth
the first philosophy.
Open your throat. Make a home
for wild silence.

LUNCH

You are picking
at the salad with
more interest
than lettuce
deserves.

The unsaid
shakes our chairs,
even as the stalk
of a bobbing daisy
in that vase holds
the line hard
between us.

At shadow's edge
of full remembering,
ache rises in your
belly, licks
at your mouth,

a word balloon
hovers
distended, sweet
menace, swells
at the very thought
of

us. Yes,
touch me.
Taste. Prick
this silence. Do it
now.

You wet your
lips, you dare
not raise
your fork.

THE NIGHT THEY WERE DANCING

Late at night when your station has gone
off the air, you still can turn the dial, still catch
strains of a hurtin' song, arcing
in, drawing
out. It's
        the atmosphere, darlin', the
waltz of old rhythms, the sway
and the ache in the twang
of a tune.
      Child,
     you
  ripped through my body,
pulled down the world, tossed me
on a bloodwave, turned me in air. Wracked
by the grace of birth's mystic fault line I was
taut, mute, left
hanging
on a wire between backbreath
and scream.
          Earth knows this
old rhythm, dials it in through the
moon. A steady beat and a
      dip,
bright skirts in
summer, dance halls
by the lake, rush
of desire turning feet turning
lives, generations of longing
pulled by the wind, dawn
dusk and dawn,
drawstring
through time. (And
no, my son,

no,
we cannot watch our feet here, cannot look
down. Limbs we kiss too soon dance
the wind, too soon rise and step
away now and
go.)   But later,
much later, the sound of your children,
a room lit by candles, a sand-peppered floor, eyes
ripe as dusk. I will feel the weight
of horizons, know that yours are now
melody, harmony and beat. We will rise,
find our feet, lean
into the centre, pulled
again by that rhythm:
                    Man
turning his mother, mother
swirling her newborn,
                         allemanding their years,
leaning into the arc,
tempo and tempus, tuning in
home.

A CHILD'S GARDEN

1

No Eden under glass,
no pastoral scene
or silent pool of green
and silver life unmarked
or dewy youth or hope like
spring running. Never
was. But see, the light
is changing, slouching
now against the edge
of day. It lurks and blinks
and watches. Takes us
by the hand around
the world. Just a second
to see what's left of paradise,
a lifetime to watch
it summerfallow.

Welcome the cyborg, Eve.
She tosses apples in the air,
eats them before
                    they fall.

2

Pulling you alive
and glistening
from the stream, they
measure you, shake
their heads. But see, your eyes,
your eyes are steady as a garden
creature, and as wise.
Small as an afterthought
     you hold me.

Blue light
from the nursing station. We spend seasons
here, different rooms every time.
Tubes in a hissing tent, a clear mask,
needles, knifeblades
pulse in the flickering light.

This is how you
incubate.
Scrubbed hands roll your
tiny form, egg
on a high steel table.
You stretch
in the light, larger,
and soon we do not
                              know you.

Your crayons now cast
across the wooden floor, abandoned
for the screen. Fingers precise,
silent as laser, you bodydance
the glass, play with light, code
images as they call you away
from home. And then you rise
erect from the bitstream,
a clear-eyed cyborg,
blood and wire,
Adam of
            another dawn.

ACCIDENT REPORT

From the top I saw
his body draw
an arc on the grey
page of sky,
did not see
        the fall.

      Ski patrollers talked
      softly to him, slid
      a plank between snow and spine,
      braced his neck, tucked blankets
      around his quaking limbs.
      Swaddled, infant
      again, his eyelids blinking,
      blinking, white
      shutters.

The ambulance driver asked what's your
favourite subject how was Christmas can you move your toes how much
air did you get on that jump anyway?

                        And I,
mother on board, stared through misted glass at miles
of pines scratching that sky into my mind, felt the cold
nib of memory etching deep black marks —
                      my child's
graceful cursive arc, long flourish
of limbs,
      pause,
          above snow.

MY SON'S FRIEND CALLING

Supper is late. Stirring the soup,
muttering, as though faster-swimming
vegetables cook more quickly, turn,
reach, first ring, cradling the phone on my shoulder,
turn again to the stove —

eh
eh-

— swing open the fridge door
rustle in the freezer for that bag
of peas where the hell —

enh, unh
is is
eh
— we are late for baseball. I toss in
the green pellets, stir, poke at slow carrots, plan
the fastest route to the field, mothermind
noting where the mitt is, the bugspray, the ball,
pour milk, gather utensils —

is-is-is-djuh ... djuh ...

Hanging the live connection on my shoulder, I place
my hand over the receiver, call out to my son:

It's for you.
It's Thomas.

Dipping the ladle in the soup, I hold
the handle of the pot, taste
cold knowledge:
I have joined the ranks of those who do not answer that boy's call.

JUSTIN

Word shoots
over teacher telegraph
through the county:
                    Justin's coming!
A file on you thick and scattered as purpled
paper in the supply room, electric
as a Stephen King story with only a little
blood, just a little
                    (well, there was that time on the playground
                    by the trees, parents called it a swarming, called
                    you an instigator, but of course, who knows what
                    the truth is).
It is June, again
you are gone, hurtling out there
toward another September, another school. Here,
the room is closed. Desks dark and rigid loom against
apparitions we cannot wipe from the board. But those stories
                                                    dangle,
crackle like live wires over the swimming hole.
                                        Justin. Street-smart and
scrappy, you had a mouth onto you, as we say
here, and quite a fist, too. And charm? Sand
to the Bedouins, ice to the Inuit and only
nine years old.

The day I brought paint and
brushes to the class, arriving just as recess
ended, carrying pails and sponges, rolls of paper, I
wasn't thinking when I set it down, all that
colour and possibility.
                    Hey! That's mine! A
yelp, a swagger. A heart
        beat.
        Justin's desk, the girl beside me whispered.
        Every muscle in the room,
alert.

I was just about to lift a pail when
    you leapt at me
        planted your face in my belly
        wiry arms pinching my
waist, wailing:

Oh painting painting painting thank you thank you thank you.

(The girl rolled her eyes: relief, perhaps, or homage
to a ham).

As your trembling fingers took a brush, your eyes
were down, lashes glistening.
We only breathed, watched you
open yellow.

THEY LEAVE HOME: ETHNOGRAPHIES

1. Near Peggy's Cove

In the circle of women, she wears
her daughter's faded No Fear sweatshirt, talks
of her passion for basketball,
her skateboard. So quick, they
thought it was just a flu that lingered.
Puffs of air from her throat —
I can't stop the tears —
She would have been fifteen this year.

2. Ingramport

At night, he wrestles
dreams, cold fingers still knotted
on the knapsack. It was enough
in the dark water to buoy him. He'd gone
back, they said, to pull one buddy to the shore, then
lay in the mud, spent, listening
to voices from the middle
of the lake calling,
     calling, the boat sunk now,
the sound of his own throat strangling
in throbs. Covered his ears with
the sodden pack, waited for the lake to swallow
their screams. One year later, I see
him on the steps of the school. His eyes are
old. I wonder if those screams
are still fresh, bright as fish
in an open boat.

3. Southwest Cove

The news report says he pled
guilty. He hated them anyway, claimed
an informant. Police confirmed
he ended the late-night quarrel
about family chores early the next
morning in their bedroom
while both were still
asleep. Two righteous
gunshots, someone said. At Annie's,
no talk of coffee or pie
or the trawler gone aground. We stare
out the window, down the road,
yellow tape rupturing the horizon. Later,
they said, his sister cried out
in the courtroom:
you are no longer my brother,
you took everything, you
are gone from me.

4. Tancook Island

Islanders do not talk about
the man with the gun. At five
in the morning, he came to his
sons' beds, left their blood on the walls, woke
his wife, then shot himself. They talk instead
of burning the house, rebuilding for her.

In the church she is silent,
asks the pastor to say only:
my boys meant everything to me.
                              Outside,
in the Tancook wind, she climbs
into the pick-up, turns the key. One boy's
coffin rides in the truck bed,
the other is transported by a friend. Taken home
up the hill, against the sun,
into the mouth of the earth.

5. VIA Rail West out of Halifax

Somewhere on the prairie,
he wakes now to the light of the East, checks
the bag we bought for his journey —
tickets, passport, gum
for his woolly mouth. The train rocks
him toward the West and mountains
and we wait at the other edge
of the country, watch the sun
rise and fall, each
ring his call,
his clear voice cutting
through the dark
roar of films that reel
behind our eyes.

LOSING HER
for Don McKay

I find her finally
in the woods beside the house.
She does not bark, only lifts her head,
groans. Her eye sends back
the porch light, sends back all our paths:
trails, beaches, Economy Mountain in spring
and fall, tide flats where once we found a seal cow
stranded. She watched in wonder
then, did not bark. Now her body bakes in fever,
she tries to rise, falls
back. She will not take food. Mosquitoes
draw to her skin. Near her grey face
a fist of tender fiddlehead opens in the air.
Cars drone in the distance. Behind us
the moon. Above, two stars

on the warmest night of spring.

The cat approaches, curls against
her burning ribs, red coat sour
with sweat. She trembles,
looks at me. Wonder, again.
Air crawls from her throat.
I lie down with her, leaves and a loon
call rub at my ears. The cat walks away.

Later that night my husband and I lay her on an old board from the shed,
carry her into the house, drip water down her throat with a baster.
A blanket does not stop her quivering.

In the glare of morning sun
she convulses for a last hour.

While her body cools we dig
into the hill, her citadel
of local knowledge. Rock under
rock, we carve a bed, try
to lower her, measure again nose to tail,
unearth more stone. Our spades crack
and clang and black flies
hover, insistent, dumb to everything but blood.

We cover her with a sheet. Her tongue hangs out of her jaw, incongruous,
comical, I cannot stuff it back. My sons toss in cubes of cheese,
I throw the first spade of clay. It rains all night.
From the deck, I watch the mound of earth turning
to mud, remember that forsythia
bloom soon.

Don't. I still hear
whimpered dreams, paws padding when the fridge opens,
sobs of welcome, tail thumps on the wood floor all those thousands
of early mornings. Still see her eyes.
Don't talk to me
about bathos.
Just show me poems about dogs.

AUGUST

On a night like this wide open silence.
Moths guard the edge of the screen
(implacable, they know more light is inside).

The grass, cold as sea water under
my bare feet, grounds me.
Nothing moves out here
but the tide, sucking back
to the centre of the earth,
balancing
moon, planet.

Inside the cabin
one child sleeps salty-eyed,
sunsoaked, with seaweed hair.
Another in the field
watches the night sky for meteor showers.

After counting yellow blossoms
on the summer squash, I lie down by the garden,
so flat against the earth I am the horizon
calling for Hesperis:

Hear my heart, I tell her.
Muscle moving in the soil,
blood washing out with the tide,
memory rising
to the moon,
                with no name
but August.

AT THE NIGHT WINDOW

Cool air rushing like water
           over the sill.
Thud and scratch of junebugs.
Beyond them a car, distant

bullet over asphalt. Turn
your face to the breeze,
inhale the chiaroscuro night.

This is your negative space, the dark
sleeve you pull yourself through by the seams,
time to imagine your dying, rebirthing, listen

to the snap of twigs on the forest floor.
Could be a waitress right now pouring cups
of ground energy, a trucker shifting down

at the exit to his bunk between gravel and trees.
Or old lovers turning, feet entwined
like roots. Somewhere, someone's last

breath, an easy sigh. Your children are upstairs,
eyelids and fingers twitching in sleep's
short-feature films. Now and then a plane

growls overhead rushing time fences, its belly
full of strangers in a pale field of sky.
You don't know where the birds are.

Here is the true half of the clock, universe to be
naked against tall grey trees, to crawl out
to the fiddleheads, uncurl them with song.

Turned away from the sun now, the world is on
backshift. Singular, unblinking, you watch it work
through the hours making dawn.

NEAR FIVE ISLANDS

Spruce trees behind the camp shed
their dry conical tips, another spring, and
                                    green sweetens.
The neighbour's chain saw whines through felled
pine down the hill. Assembling a small house
for the orphaned adult son, the one made simple,
they say, in a car wreck twenty years ago.
Sara's house up for sale and, down the cove, brothers and sisters
hold their ground, knotted in roots
of wrongs now overgrown, too thick to untangle.

We have tried to fix the cabin deck with old bricks,
a decaying pole. Years of heavy snow, one end totters,
the roof sags. Do we stay,
rebuild? Go?
                    At dusk,
the tide begins its nocturnal hiss, bats swoop
low across the field, searchlights
for insects. In the bay the moon walks
across water to the islands below Kenomee Mountain.
This water remembers Glooscap's wrath. Just watch when it's high
under the new moon. It speaks in whole trees, erupts in boulders, its rising
claws rip the face off cliffs, unwrap red earth on their way down, offer up
a fossil now and then. This water is the language
of M'iqmaq tales, June constellations.

Don't bother it with details.

LOON SONG: SEPTEMBER

Pull your rope
over water rocking
in longing, slide between
rasping limbs of pines,
tug through churning dreams,
sticky harvest frenzy, loop along
the hillside, up & up, in
slender air this cool night,
slip through the open screen
into this green-licked copper shell,
knotted by grief, pull, pull, & ring
this heart
this bell.

HOME STRETCH

Febrile air, Portage la Prairie PetroCan
and the restaurant boarded up. Only a till,
a restroom. Trucks swarm like flies
around the rich draw of pumps
and on the east side, in shade,
a shiny hog, black as a roach
and a biker's tan body stroked by shredded jeans.
He holds a lighter at the end of a long brown
fresco of tattoo and leans toward the
woman's tiny frame,
his ponytail whipping in the fetid exhalation
of traffic on the Trans-Canada, this long
hot summer road. Snaps
his thumb, flame pops out like a tongue.
She curls around it, curves into a promise
of smoke, late afternoon hit, one of the few remaining
pleasures, she always says. Her hair white
as stripped bone, too near the flame I notice,
and her hand shakes, steady now, steady, the glare
of prairie sky beyond glancing off her shades —
We're pariahs, you know.

She spits it out like a blown piston, barks
her Dunhill-and-scotch laugh and the trucker
at the pump nearby startles, notes
the rumpled face, white cane, body like
a divining rod, tremulous and twisting,

but grounded.
She nods her thanks, the biker
smiles, they are nose to nose now —
We get it where we can, you bet.
They giggle, inhale with satisfaction.

I have emerged from the restroom
into the fullness of the sun and waited within earshot until
she has tossed the smouldering inch
next to the Harley wheel. He flicks his next
to hers. They look out beyond the shimmer of road
ahead, huddled,
silence reaching.

I join them, grind the fires out with my heel
and they look at me as through a dream. Smile.

Take it easy now: whisper, fingers light on her
sleeve. My mother grins at us, gives me her arm,
warm and fragile as ash, lifts her cane
in salute and we open the door
for the last leg home.

GATHERING WINTER FUEL

Winter thickens. Crows retreat with the sun. House settles
in shudders, a lumbering creature circling dusk. Night is darker

now, air sharp as glass. Kitchen window hangs flat and white,
lighting your walk, crisp and even to the woodshed. Cat dives from

the cooling hood of the car, creeps like spilled ink toward you, pooling
at your feet. Working at the pile, you pull logs from the end, inhale

the whine of pine gum, feel the pok of cold wood striking wood. Trees in
your arms, food for a hungry fire. Above, stars are ice, they fail your heart,

you know not how. Brightly shining moon, though the frost is cruel.
Cat, like your page, treads in your footsteps beside the forest

fence. Where the snow lay dinted, gestures, dance of warm lit bones,
your bodies leagues of artery wrapped in skin and fur, and the cold

is roundabout, deep and crisp. Mark your footsteps boldly.
A rude wind rises, wild lament. And bitter weather. Thickening, as blood.

NOW

that spiders sew
the wanton yard to itself,
tomatoes dangle in green
forlorn fists, and birds
swoop from sly and ardent claws
of cats lurking below
the bush at dusk,
        now
that light is more
like paint and less
like curiosity,

let's boil the garden in glass
bottles, transform it
to ice, store yesterday
under *almost*,
beside *if only*.

Gather all the songs:
hummingbird,
feet sweeping sand,
trickling blue juice,
simmer of crickets,
swagger of basil,
sunset calliope,
Longing.

Wear them like a veil.

Over the screen door,
the steely face of winter
fastens
like a nail.

CAST OFF

Dark warm sea and coil of blood and breath that brought you here,
faith in their presence at your crib before your tongue knows

how to name, sweet sop of biscuits slipped from your wet grip,
clasp of guiding hands, firm legs of kitchen chairs and the gingered

breath of your dog. He won't come back. Belief that words
will give you what you ask, whispers of your schoolyard mates

whose maypole orbits leave you bereft in space. Let go of these. While
you're at it, first supple brush of mouth on mouth, hot satin of his belly

on your own, all the masks you were until you saw your face, plans
to build your own retreat, raise the perfect child, save black sheep in your

family, start over, redeem, forget. Prayers for rain. Disguises. Windows.
Veils. Let them go. Let go the certainty that what you water dig bend turn feed

mould touch tend will root and thrive and tendril the planet,
long endure and long stitch years into years ahead. Let go.

Acknowledgements

Some of these poems have appeared in different versions in *CV2, Grain, The Malahat Review, The Antigonish Review, Room of One's Own, The Grist Mill, Language Arts,* as well as in *Madwoman in the Academy* (University of Calgary Press), *Child* (Boundary Bay Press), *Wayfaring* (Harrish Press) and *Not Just Any Dress: Explorations of Dress, Identity, and the Body,* Sandra Weber and Claudia Mitchell, editors (Peter Lang Publishing Group). My thanks to all the editors.

Many thanks to the participants, faculty and staff of the Banff Centre for the Arts' 2001 Studio, Banff Centre 2002 Wired Writing Studio, and the 2002 Sage Hill Writing Experience. I am grateful to Sage Hill for the Anne Szumigalski Scholarship, and to the Banff Centre for financial support to attend. Special thanks to Don McKay, Jan Zwicky, Sue Goyette, Betsy Warland, Christopher Wiseman, Dennis Lee, and Carmelita McGrath for their supportive and astute guidance as these poems developed.

For their inspiration and enthusiasm, I thank Daphne Marlatt, Joan Clark, Bernadette Wagner, Liz Zetlin, George Sipos, Carl Leggo, Lindsay Brown, Verlie Wile, Arlene Connell, Liz Garland, Marilyn Fedderson, Pat Clifford, Sharon Carson, Lekkie Hopkins, CAIR and Backalong colleagues, the Yarker Circle, Mary Jane Copps, Joanne Jefferson, and the Oxford Writing Collective. I am especially grateful to Joan and the Rogersville group for starting the fire, and to Don McKay for kindling. Thanks also to Jane Buss and the Writers' Federation of Nova Scotia, David Rimmington and The Economy Shoe Shop, and Jeanette Lynes, her students, and the B2G Café.

Stan Dragland's ability to listen under the words taught me much. Spirited, sharp, and generous, Stan is the single malt of editors. Thanks to the tireless poet-publisher Joe Blades, and to the judges of the 2003 Poets' Corner Award, for making this book possible.

Allan, David, and Jesse — gifts beyond measure — my heartfelt thanks.

The book's epigraph is taken from *The Stubborn Particulars of Grace* by Bronwen Wallace (McClelland & Stewart, 1987, p. 109).

"The Dress, from Here" is in response to C.K. Williams' poem, "The Dress", published in *Repair* (Farrar, Straus, and Giroux, 1999).

A Selection of Our Titles in Print

A Fredericton Alphabet (John Leroux) photos, architecture, ISBN 1-896647-77-4
All the Perfect Disguises (Lorri Neilsen Glenn) poetry, 1-55391-010-9
Antimatter (Hugh Hazelton) poetry, 1-896647-98-7
Avoidance Tactics (Sky Gilbert) drama, 1-896647-50-2
Bathory (Moynan King) drama, 1-896647-36-7
Break the Silence (Denise DeMoura) poetry, 1-896647-87-1
Combustible Light (Matt Santateresa) poetry, 0-921411-97-9
Crossroads Cant (Mary Elizabeth Grace, Mark Seabrook, Shafiq, Ann Shin, Joe Blades, editor) poetry, 0-921411-48-0
Cuerpo amado/ Beloved Body (Nela Rio; Hugh Hazelton, translator) poetry, 1-896647-81-2
Dark Seasons (Georg Trakl; Robin Skelton, translator) poetry, 0-921411-22-7
Day of the Dog-tooth Violets (Christina Kilbourne) fiction, 0-921411-44-8
During Nights That Undress Other Nights/ En las noches que desvisten otras noches (Nela Rio; Elizabeth Gamble Miller, translator) poetry, 1-55391-008-7
for a cappuccino on Bloor (kath macLean) poetry, 0-921411-74-X
Great Lakes logia (Joe Blades, editor) art & writing anthology, 1-896647-70-7
Heart-Beat of Healing (Denise DeMoura) poetry, 0-921411-24-3
Heaven of Small Moments (Allan Cooper) poetry, 0-921411-79-0
Herbarium of Souls (Vladimir Tasic) short fiction, 0-921411-72-3
I Hope It Don't Rain Tonight (Phillip Igloliorti) poetry, 0-921411-57-X
Jive Talk: George Fetherling in Interviews and Documents (Joe Blades, editor), 1-896647-54-5
Mangoes on the Maple Tree (Uma Parameswaran) fiction, 1-896647-79-0
Manitoba highway map (rob mclennan) poetry, 0-921411-89-8
Paper Hotel (rob mclennan) poetry, 1-55391-004-4
Railway Station (karl wendt) poetry, 0-921411-82-0
Reader Be Thou Also Ready (Robert James) fiction, 1-896647-26-X
resume drowning (Jon Paul Fiorentino) poetry, 1-896647-94-4
Rum River (Raymond Fraser) fiction, 0-921411-61-8
Shadowy:Technicians: New Ottawa Poets (rob mclennan, editor), poetry, 0-921411-71-5
Singapore (John Palmer) drama, 1-896647-85-5
Song of the Vulgar Starling (Eric Miller) poetry, 0-921411-93-6
Speaking Through Jagged Rock (Connie Fife) poetry, 0-921411-99-5
Starting from Promise (Lorne Dufour) poetry, 1-896647-52-9
Sunset (Pablo Urbanyi; Hugh Hazelton, translator) fiction, 1-55391-014-1
Sweet Mother Prophesy (Andrew Titus) fiction, 1-55391-002-8
Tales for an Urban Sky (Alice Major) poetry, 1-896647-11-1
The Longest Winter (Julie Doiron, Ian Roy) photos, short fiction, 0-921411-95-2
This Day Full of Promise (Michael Dennis) poetry, 1-896647-48-0
The Sweet Smell of Mother's Milk-Wet Bodice (Uma Parameswaran) fiction, 1-896647-72-3
The Yoko Ono Project (Jean Yoon) drama, 1-55391-001-X
Túnel de proa verde/ Tunnel of the Green Prow (Nela Rio; Hugh Hazelton, translator) poetry, 0-921411-80-4
What Was Always Hers (Uma Parameswaran) short fiction, 1-896647-12-X

www.brokenjaw.com hosts our current catalogue, submissions guidelines, manuscript award competitions, booktrade sales representation and distribution information. Broken Jaw Press eBooks of selected titles are available from http://www.PublishingOnline.com. Directly from us, all individual orders must be prepaid. All Canadian orders must add 7% GST/HST (Canada Customs and Revenue Agency Number: 12489 7943 RT0001).

BROKEN JAW PRESS, Box 596 Stn A, Fredericton NB E3B 5A6, Canada